Songs and Prayers from Taizé

Songs and Prayers from Taizé

GEOFFREY
CHAPMAN
MOWBRAY

Geoffrey Chapman Mowbray
A Cassell imprint
Villiers House, 41/47 Strand, London WC2N 5JE, England

First published 1991
Reprinted 1991

British Library Cataloguing in Publication Data
Songs and prayers from Taizé
  1. Christianity: Public worship
  242.8

ISBN 0-264-67256-9
     0-264-67265-8 (10-pack)

Cover illustration © S. Nitzschke, Dresden

Music: J. Berthier, M. Praetorius (song 23), S. Toolan (song 25)

The English-language versions of the songs which appear in this
book come from various sources. Some of them began their life in
Asia, some were written or revised in the USA, others have been
part of the repertoire in Taizé for a number of years.

Text and music set by Linda Lancaster

Printed and bound in Great Britain by
Hollen Street Press Limited, Slough

CONTENTS

Preparing a time of prayer

The elements contained in this booklet can be used separately or combined in different ways. They can be used for a time of prayer with other people, for personal meditation or as part of a regular service of worship.

During Sunday morning worship in a parish or congregation, meditative songs are particularly appropriate after the readings, during the communion or at the very end.

A group of people can use the following order to pray together:

One or two opening songs	
A psalm (with alleluia)	9–14
Song of light (optional)	15
First Bible reading	16–19
Song	
Second Bible reading (optional)	16–19
Song	
Silence	20
Prayer of intercession or adoration	21–28
Our Father	
Concluding prayer	29–34
Meditative songs	
Prayer around the Cross (optional) or	35–36
Celebration of the resurrection (optional)	36

From the depths of the human condition a secret
aspiration rises up. Caught up in the anonymous
rhythms of schedules and timetables, men and
women of today are implicitly thirsting for the one
essential reality: an inner life, signs of the invisible.

Nothing is more conducive to a communion with
the living God than a meditative common prayer
with, as its high point, singing that never ends and
that continues in the silence of one's heart when one is
alone again. When the mystery of God becomes
tangible through the simple beauty of symbols, when
it is not smothered by too many words, then a
common prayer, far from exuding monotony and
boredom, awakens us to heaven's joy on earth.

To celebrate such an inclusive common prayer, only
a few people are needed, sometimes just two or three
young adults. Already, through them, a sign of Christ
becomes visible. And in addition, if young people
were to join, at least once a week, the prayer of the
local Christian community, a Sunday morning
worship service involving all the generations, from
little children to elderly persons, then the universality
of fellowship in Christ would find a clear expression.

In a technological society, there is a clear separation between prayer and work. When inner life and human solidarity appear to be in competition with one another, as if people had to choose between them, that opposition tears apart the very depths of the soul.

Prayer is a serene force at work within human beings, stirring them up, transforming them, never allowing them to close their eyes in the face of evil, of wars, of all that threatens the weak of this world. From it we draw the energy to wage other struggles — to enable our loved ones to survive, to transform the human condition, to make the earth a place fit to live in.

All who walk in the footsteps of Christ, while being in the presence of God, remain alongside other people as well. They do not separate prayer and commitment.

Brother Roger of Taizé

Psalms

One or two persons can read or sing the verses of a
Psalm* while everyone sings a response after each
verse, for example an Alleluia (no. 1, 2 or 3).

Alleluia
— I will bless the Lord at all times
   on my lips, the sound of his praise.
Alleluia
— Give glory, my soul, to the Lord,
   all the humble, hear and rejoice.
Alleluia
— Come, let us worship the Lord,
   with one voice give glory to God.
Alleluia
— I cried to the Lord, he replied,
   he freed me when I was afraid.
Alleluia
— With God is the fullness of joys,
   turn to him, you will not be deceived;
Alleluia
— When the poor cry out, he gives heed,
   he is close to all in distress.
Alleluia

from Psalm 34

---

* When Psalms are used for prayer, it is important to select only
verses which are easily accessible.

Like a deer that yearns
for a cooling stream
so my soul is athirst
for you, my God.

My soul is thirsting for God,
for the living God;
when shall I come and behold
the face of God?

Tears are my only food
by night and by day;
always I hear them say:
Where is your God?

Once I went with the throng
to the House of our God,
with shouts of rejoicing and praise
on the lips of the crowd.

What weighs you down, my soul?
Why faint in my breast?
Hope in God: I will praise him still,
my Saviour, my God.

from Psalm 42

God, you are my God, I seek your face at dawn,
my soul is thirsting for you,
my body is pining for you,
parched ground, waterless and dry;
in the Sanctuary, I long to adore you,
to behold your glory and power.

Your love is better than life,
my lips will proclaim your praise;
all my life, I would bless you,
my hands lifted up in prayer;
my soul feasting till satisfied,
joy on my lips, praise in my mouth.

When I think of you, as I sleep,
remember you all through the night;
you have been my help,
I rejoice in the shadow of your wings;
my soul finds rest at your side,
your right hand is holding me safe.

from Psalm 63

To you, Lord, I shall always stay near,
you hold me by your right hand;
you lead me by your counsel,
and will draw me in the wake of your glory.

Whom else do I have in heaven?
With you, I desire nothing on earth;
my heart and my flesh may dissolve
but God is for ever my portion, my rock.

It is good to draw close to God,
I have made the Lord my refuge,
and now I will tell of all your works.

from Psalm 73

See, how my heart is full of longing
for the House of God.

My soul is pining and sighs
with longing for the House of the Lord;
my heart and my flesh sing: Joy!
to you, O Living God.

For the sparrows have found a house,
and the swallows a nest for their young:
your altar, God of all the worlds,
you, my King and my God.

How bless'd are all who live in your House,
for ever and ever they adore;
happy those whose strength is in you,
hearts strong for the climb to your throne.

They must go through the Valley of Thorns,
but they find it a place of springs;
they advance from strength to strength,
God will appear to them in Zion.

Lord God, listen to my prayer,
give heed, O Jacob's God;
Lord, our Shield, behold,
and look upon the face of your Christ.

For me, one day in your courts
is better than a thousand elsewhere;
the doorway of the House of my God,
no longer the house of the wicked.

For God is our Sun and our Shield,
he gives us glory and grace;
the Lord refuses no good things
to those whose hearts are true.

Lord of hosts, God almighty,
happy, who trusts in you!

from Psalm 84

O sing a new song to the Lord,
for the wonders he has wrought;
for the victory his hand has gained,
his holiness of power.

The Lord has shown that he will save,
in the sight of the nations revealing his power,
ever mindful of his kindness and truth
for the people he loves.

All the ends of the earth have seen
the salvation of our God;
sing out for the Lord, all the earth,
exult in hymns of joy.

Sing praises to God with the harp,
with instruments and songs;
blow high the trumpets and horns,
extol the Lord our King.

Seas and the deep, give voice!
With the world and all its throngs;
let the rivers clap their hands,
all the hills shout for joy!

Before the Lord, for he comes,
he comes to judge the earth,
with justice, he will rule the world,
all peoples, with his truth.

from Psalm 98

Give glory to God, all the earth
and worship the Lord with cheerful songs,
go up to him, repeating shouts of joy.

Remember that the Lord is God,
for he made us, the work of his hands,
his people and the sheep of his flock.

So come into his gates, giving thanks,
and enter his courts with songs of praise,
bring him thanks, sing praise to his name.

See, how the Lord is good!
See, for eternity his love!
He is faithful, age after age!

from Psalm 100

Give praise to the Lord, O my soul,
all my being, praise his holy name,
give praise to the Lord, O my soul,
remember the kindnesses of God.

The Lord will pardon all your misdeeds,
he will heal you of every kind of ill,
he will rescue your life from the grave,
and will crown you with his kindness and love;
he comes to fill you with every kind of good,
and like an eagle, your youth will remain.

For the Lord is a righteous judge,
he brings justice for all the oppressed,
he revealed to Moses his ways,
to the children of Israel his deeds.

The Lord our God is compassion and love,
slow to anger, abounding in concern;
he will not chide us until we despair,
his anger is not destined to endure;
he does not treat us according to our sins,
nor repay us as our ways would deserve.

As high as the sky above the earth,
so the Lord, for all who love him, is kind,
as the east is far from the west,
so far he removes all our sins.

from Psalm 103

I lift up my eyes to the hills:
where is my help to come from?
My help comes from the Lord,
who made both heaven and earth.

He will not let you stumble or fall,
your guardian will not sleep.
No, as the guardian of his people,
he never falls asleep.

The Lord is your guardian and your shade,
he stays close at hand;
the sun will not strike you by day,
nor the moon by night.

The Lord will keep you from harm
he watches over your life;
the Lord watches over you as you come and go,
both now and for evermore.

from Psalm 121

The Magnificat (Song of Mary)

My soul sings praises to the Lord,
my spirit rejoices in God my Saviour,
for he has been mindful of his humble servant;
henceforth all generations will call me blessed.

The Almighty has done great things for me;
holy is his name.
His mercy stretches from age to age
upon those who revere him.

He has put forth his arm in strength
scattering the proud-hearted.
He has cast down the mighty from their thrones
and lifted up the lowly.

He has filled the hungry with good things,
he has sent the rich away empty-handed.

He has helped his servant Israel
ever remembering his love,
the love he promised to our ancestors,
to Abraham and his children for ever.

The song of light

Christians in some parts of Asia have discovered an appealing symbol for the beginning of evening prayer, a symbol that can easily be used in other parts of the world. A song celebrating the light of Christ is sung (no. 36 or 37) and, during it, some young people or children, holding lighted tapers, come up to light an oil lamp set on a lampstand. The symbol reminds us that, even when we are shrouded in darkness, in our personal life or in the life of humanity, Christ's love is a fire that never dies out.

Bible readings

Choose one or two readings which are not too long and do not require explanation.*

Old Testament

Genesis 12.1–5	The call of Abraham
Deuteronomy 30.11–14	The word of God is very near you.
1 Samuel 3.1–10	The Lord calls Samuel.
1 Kings 17.8–16	The widow of Zarephath
1 Kings 19.9–13a	Elijah waits for the Lord on Mount Horeb.
Proverbs 4.18–23	Keep watch over your heart: it is the wellspring of life.
Isaiah 11.1–9	Peace on earth
Isaiah 40.27–31	Those who hope in the Lord will renew their strength.
Isaiah 43.18–21	The Lord says: Do not dwell upon the past. See, I am doing something new.
Isaiah 44.21–23	The Lord says: I have swept away your sins like the morning mist.
Isaiah 58.5–11	If you do away with injustice, your night will become like the light of day.
Jeremiah 1.4–8	The call of Jeremiah
Jeremiah 29.11–13	The Lord says: you will find me when you seek me with all your heart
Jeremiah 31.31–34	A new Covenant
Ezekiel 36.24–28	The Lord says: I will give you a new heart.
Micah 6.6, 8	Act justly and walk humbly with your God.

---

* In order to have a more complete choice, the **Letter from Taizé**, published every two months, gives a sentence of Scripture with a corresponding reference to a longer passage for every day of the year.

Gospel

Matthew 5.1–12	The Beatitudes
Matthew 6.25–34	Do not worry about your life. Seek first the Kingdom and its righteousness.
Matthew 7.7–11	Ask, and it will be given to you. Seek, and you will find.
Matthew 11.25–30	Jesus said: Come to me, for I am gentle and humble in heart, and you will find rest.
Matthew 13.44–46	The parables of the treasure and the Pearl
Matthew 16.13–20	Peter's profession of faith
Matthew 16.21–28	Jesus said: Anyone who loses their life for my sake will find it.
Matthew 21.28–31	The parable of the two sons
Mark 1.9–20	The call of the first disciples
Mark 2.13–17	Jesus said: I have not come to call the righteous, but sinners.
Mark 4.26–29	The Kingdom of God is like a seed that sprouts and grows, without us knowing how.
Mark 6.30–44	The feeding of the five thousand
Mark 10.13–16	The Kingdom of God belongs to those who are like children.
Mark 10.17–30	Leaving all to follow Jesus
Luke 1.26–45	The call of Mary
Luke 6.27–38	Love your enemies. Do not judge.
Luke 9.57–62	The cost of following Jesus
Luke 10.25–37	The good Samaritan
Luke 10.38–42	Martha and Mary
Luke 15.11-32	The prodigal son

Luke 17.20–21	The Kingdom of God is within you.
Luke 19.1–10	Zacchaeus
Luke 23.33–49	The Crucifixion
Luke 24.1–8	The Resurrection
Luke 24.13–35	The Risen Christ on the road to Emmaus
John 3.1–8	Nicodemus
John 4.1–15	Jesus and the Samaritan woman
John 6.66–69	Lord, to whom shall we go? You have the words of eternal life.
John 10.7–15	The Good Shepherd
John 13.1–15	Jesus washes his disciples' feet.
John 14.1–4	Do not let your hearts be troubled.
John 14.27–29	The peace of Christ
John 15.9–12	Love one another.
John 20.1–10	The Resurrection
John 20.11–18	Jesus appears to Mary Magdalene.
John 21.15–19	The Risen Christ with Peter

Epistle

Acts 2.42–47 and Acts 4.32–35	The community of the first believers
Romans 8.14–17	The Spirit who says: Abba, Father!
Romans 8.22–29	God's Spirit prays in us.

1 Corinthians 12.12–17, 27	The Body of Christ
1 Corinthians 13	Love will never fail.
2 Corinthians 4.5–10	We bear the treasure of the Gospel in jars of clay to show it comes from God and not from us.
2 Corinthians 4.16–18	We fix our eyes not on what is seen, but what is unseen.
2 Corinthians 5.16–20	God has entrusted to us the message of reconciliation.
Galatians 2.20	I no longer live, but Christ lives in me.
Galatians 3.26–4.7	You are all sons of God, you are all one in Christ Jesus.
Ephesians 3.14–19	May you know the love of Christ which surpasses all understanding.
Ephesians 4.1–6	Keep the unity of the Spirit through the bond of peace.
Philippians 3.7–14	Everything is a loss compared with the surpassing greatness of knowing Christ Jesus.
Philippians 4.4–7	Rejoice in the Lord! Do not be anxious about anything.
Colossians 2.9–13	We have already been raised with Christ.
Colossians 3.12–17	Forgive as the Lord forgave you.
1 Thessalonians 5.14–24	Pray at all times, give thanks in all circumstances.
Hebrews 12.1–3	Let us throw off sin that so easily entangles, and fix our eyes on Jesus.
James 1.12–18	God does not tempt anyone.
1 Peter 1.3–9	Though you have not seen Christ, you love him.
1 Peter 4.12–14	Suffering with Christ
1 John 3.1–3	We are children of God!
1 John 3.18–20	If our heart condemn us, God is greater than our heart.
1 John 4.7–12	This is love: not that we loved God, but that he loved us and sent his Son for our forgiveness.
Revelation 22.1–5	The servants of God will see his face.

Silence

When we try to express communion with God in words, we rapidly reach the end of our capacities. But in the depths of our being Christ is praying, far more than we imagine. Compared to the immensity of that hidden prayer of Christ in us, our explicit praying dwindles to almost nothing. That is why silence is so essential in discovering the heart of prayer.*

Although God never stops trying to communicate with us, God never wants to impose anything on us. Often God's voice comes in a whisper, in a breath of silence. Remaining in silence in God's presence, open to the Spirit, is already prayer.

It is not a matter of trying to obtain inner silence at all costs by following some method that creates a kind of emptiness within. The important thing is a childlike attitude of trust by which we allow Christ to pray within us silently, and then one day, we will discover that the depths of our being are inhabited by a Presence.

---

* It is best to have just one fairly long period of silence (5–10 minutes) during the prayer, rather than several shorter ones. If those taking part in the prayer are not used to silence, it is good to explain it beforehand. Or after the song immediately preceding the silence you can say, 'The prayer will now continue with a few moments of silence'.

Prayers of Intercession and Adoration

This prayer can be introduced by singing Kyrie eleison (no. 4, 5 or 6), 'Lord, have mercy', or a response from the Russian Orthodox tradition, Gospodi pomiluj (no. 7), 'Lord, have compassion'. These or other suitable responses can be repeated after each intercession.*

Intercession: prayer for all humanity

Kyrie eleison (or Gospodi pomiluj)
— O Christ, your life was not spectacular: you
  carried a cross: help us walk along your road . . .
Kyrie eleison (or Gospodi pomiluj)
— O Christ, you learned faithfulness by suffering:
  you have become a source of eternal salvation . . .
Kyrie eleison
— O Christ, when wounded you did not make
  threats: show us how to forgive to the very end . . .

---

* After the written petitions are finished, time may be left for people to pray spontaneously in their own words, with everyone joining to sing Kyrie eleison after each prayer. These spontaneous prayers should be brief and be addressed to God; they should not become an excuse for expressing one's own ideas and opinions to other people by formulating them as a prayer.

Kyrie eleison
— O Christ, when forced to suffer you did not rebel:
  transfigure our refusals . . .
Kyrie eleison
— O Christ, you see our suffering and failures: help
  us walk along your road . . .
Kyrie eleison
— O Christ, you see the pain of the exiled and the
  abandoned: take their suffering upon yourself . . .
Kyrie eleison
— O Christ, when lies and worries tempt us
  to forsake you, your Holy Spirit remains always
  within us . . .
Kyrie eleison
— O Christ, when our hearts become heavy, make
  them transparent like a springtime in flower . . .
Kyrie eleison
— O Christ, you bring happiness to your servants:
  enable us to live lives rooted in your trust . . .
Kyrie eleison
— O Christ, our life is hidden with you in God; your
  joy penetrates to the depths of our souls . . .
Kyrie eleison

or

— Loving Father, you have sent the Spirit of your
  Son into our hearts . . .

— Jesus, Son of God, you asked that your Church
  receive the Spirit to strengthen it in faith: make us
  attentive to your Word . . .

— Jesus, Son of God, you guide your Church at all times
by the same Spirit: make us attentive to your Word . . .

— Jesus, risen from the dead, you open for us a road
towards you and towards others, even when all
ways seem closed: make us attentive to your Word . . .

— Jesus, our brother, you are with all who suffer:
comfort them by your Word . . .

— Jesus, our brother, you send us in your name to
those who need your consolation: make us
attentive to your Presence . . .

— Spirit of the living God, you renew your Church
by offering us a springtime of reconciliations:
guide us by your Word . . .

— Spirit of the living God, you cause your fruits to
ripen in our hearts: make us attentive to your Word . . .

— You grant us serene joy and peace of heart . . .

or

— Lord our God, as evening falls and the light
disappears: receive our prayer . . .

— God our Father, you look upon us with
compassion: receive our prayer . . .

— God our Father, you take upon yourself our
burdens: fill us with your peace . . .

— God our Father, in silence we are led to you:
sustain us by your Word . . .

— God our Father, your love is all we need: welcome us and all those you have entrusted to us . . .

— God our Father, kindle a new brightness in our night: may your light shine on us . . .

or

— Lord, you make your peace shine out in our midst: may our hearts sing your praises forever . . .

— Lord, your love comes to liberate our lives: may our hearts sing your praises forever . . .

— For the Church, ferment of communion: Lord, make your face shine upon her . . .

— For a road of justice and freedom, for the leaders of the nations: Lord, may all nations give you thanks . . .

— For all believers, witnesses to hope: make your face shine upon us . . .

— For the victims of injustice and violence, for those who give aid to them: in them your praise forever . . .

— For all who give their life because of Christ and the Gospel: in them your praise forever . . .

— For all you have entrusted to us: in them your praise forever . . .

— Eternal God, you created us in your image and you saved us through your Son Jesus: look with compassion upon the entire human family . . .

— Eternal God, source of justice and peace, establish peace among the nations, the fruit of your salvation: may all peoples sing your praises . . .

— Eternal God, your love brings healing to our hatred and our sadness: bring peace to your church, to the nations . . . , to families . . . and bring inner peace to each of us . . .

— Eternal God, your Spirit of life dwells within every human being: may the Spirit enable us to tear down walls of mistrust and of fear . . .

— Christ Jesus, you came to proclaim the joyful news of peace: help us bring an end to deprivation, poverty and oppression in our societies . . .

— Eternal God, you bless every nation on this earth: remember . . . , remember those who suffer from violence and discord . . .

— Eternal God, you walk alongside the people of every land: show the leaders of nations how to follow the road of justice and of peace . . .

— Christ Jesus, you wish to reconcile the whole human race: teach us to welcome refugees and immigrants . . . to form with them a single people that belongs to you . . .

— Eternal God, by your Son Jesus Christ, you bring down the walls of separation between people: reconcile us in your Love . . .

or

— Jesus Christ, you come to transfigure us in the image of your Father and our Father: open for us the gates of your Kingdom . . .

— Jesus Christ, Light of our hearts, you know how thirsty we are: open for us the gates of your Kingdom . . .

— Jesus Christ, Light of the world, you shine for us all: enable us to discern your presence in every human being . . .

— Jesus Christ, beloved Son of the Father: inspire in us a love that is self-giving . . .

— Jesus Christ, Source of life, rest for the weary: open for us all the gates of praise . . .

— Jesus Christ, Friend of the poor: open in us the gates of simplicity to welcome you . . .

— Jesus Christ, Presence of the living God, through your Church you prepare your way for others: open for all the gates of your Kingdom . . .

— Jesus Christ, Source of peace, bring us peace of heart and peace in the world . . .

— Jesus Christ, so much greater than our hearts: in you the road to the Kingdom opens up for us . . .

Two prayers of Adoration

— O Jesus Christ, born in humility to raise up the humble,

— You lived among us, healing the sick, proclaiming Good News to the poor and freedom to prisoners,

— Jesus, you are kind and forgiving, you carry for us all that is more than we can bear,

— Jesus, gentle and humble of heart, you call all who toil and are burdened,

— You came to loose the chains of every captivity, friend of the poor, bread of hungry hearts,

— You came into the world not to be served but to serve and give your life.

— Jesus, by your resurrection from the dead you live for ever, to walk with us on the road to your Father and our Father.

— O Christ, in your resurrection you have destroyed
sin and death.

— O Christ, in your resurrection you have brought
all humanity from death to life.

— O Christ, in your resurrection you spoke joyful
news to the women and the apostles, and
salvation for the whole world.

— O Christ, in your resurrection you breathed the
Holy Spirit upon your disciples.

— O Christ, in your resurrection you promised to be
with us to the end of time.

— O Christ, in your resurrection you sent out your
apostles to the ends of the earth.

— O Christ, in your resurrection you are the
beginning, the Firstborn from among the dead.

— O Christ, in your resurrection you reconcile all
things on earth and in heaven.

Concluding Prayers

O Risen Christ, you go down
to the lowest depths
of our human condition,
and you burden yourself
with what burdens us.
Still more, you even go
to visit those who have died
without being able to know you.

And even when within us
we can hear no refrain
of your presence,
you are there.
Through your Holy Spirit
you remain within us.

Holy Spirit, Spirit of the Living God,
you breathe in us
on all that is inadequate and fragile.

You make living water spring even
from our hurts themselves. And
through you, the valley of tears
becomes a place of wellsprings.

So, in an inner life
with neither beginning nor end,
your continual presence
makes new freshness break through.

Christ, Saviour of every life, you come to us always.
Welcoming you in the peace of our nights, in the silence of
our days, in the beauty of creation, in the hours of intense
combat, welcoming you means knowing that you will be with us
in every situation, always.

Christ Jesus, even if we had faith enough to move
mountains, without living charity, what would we be?
  You love us.
Without your Holy Spirit who lives in our hearts,
what would we be?
  You love us.
Taking everything upon yourself, you open for us a way
towards faith, towards trust in God, who wants neither
suffering nor human distress.
  Spirit of the Risen Christ, Spirit of compassion,
Spirit of praise, your love for each one of us will
never disappear.

Jesus, risen Lord, at times you see me bewildered, like a stranger
on this earth. But a thirst fills my soul, the longing for your
presence. And my heart finds no rest until it can lay in you, Christ,
what was weighing it down and keeping it far from you.

Risen Christ, you take us with our hearts just as they are.
Why think we must wait for our hearts to be changed before
we go to you? You transfigure them.

With our thorns, you light a fire. The open wound in us
is the place through which your love comes streaming. And
within the very hurts themselves, you bring to fruition a
communion with you. Your voice comes to rend our night, and
the gateways of praise open up within us.

Why did I hesitate, asking for time to look after my own affairs?
Once I had put my hand to the plough, why did I look back?

And yet, though I had never seen you, I loved you, perhaps
not as I would have liked to, but I did love you.

Christ Jesus, you were suggesting to me, 'Live the very
little of the Gospel that you have understood; proclaim my life
among humanity; come and follow me'.

Until one day, returning to the source, I understood. You
were asking me to commit myself to the point of no return.

Although within us there are wounds,
Lord Christ, above all there is
the miracle of your mysterious presence.
Thus, made lighter or even set free,
we are going with you, the Christ,
from one discovery to another.

Breath of the Spirit of God,
you place faith within each one of us,
faith which is such a simple trust in you
that it is possible for all to receive it.
Without us yet being able to see clearly,
you enlighten within, O Christ,
even in the opaque regions of our being.

O God, we praise you
for the multitudes of women, men,
young people and children, who
are seeking to be witnesses of
peace, trust, and reconciliation
throughout the world.

In the footsteps of the holy witnesses
of all the ages, since Mary and the apostles.
to the believers of today,
grant us to prepare ourselves inwardly,
day after day, to place our trust
in the mystery of faith.

In following you, O Christ,
we choose to love and not to harden our hearts,
even when the incomprehensible happens.
As we remain in your presence with perseverance,
day after day, and pray with simplicity of heart,
you come and make us into people
who are a leaven of confident trust by the way we
    live.
And all that your Gospel calls us to,
all that you ask of us, you give.

Lord Christ, you see us
sometimes strangers on the earth,
taken aback by the violence,
by the harshness of oppositions.

And you come to send out a gentle breeze
on the dry ground of our doubts,
and so prepare us to be bearers
of peace and of reconciliation.

O Christ,
you take upon yourself all our burdens
so that freed of all that weighs us down,
we can constantly begin anew to walk
with lightened step,
from worry towards trusting.
from the shadows towards the clear flowing water,
from our own will towards the vision of the coming
    Kingdom.
And then we know,
though we had hardly dared hope it,
that you offer to make every human being
a reflection of your face.

Risen Jesus,
you are there close beside each person,
you descend to where we are,
to the very lowest point of our human condition,
And you take upon yourself all that hurts us,
both in ourselves and in others.
You accompany every human being.
More than that,
you visit even those who, as non-believers, have
died without having been able to know you.
And so, in our inner struggle,
the contemplation of your forgiveness
gives rise to a radiant goodness
in the humble heart that allows itself to be led
by your Spirit.

Christ Jesus, by your Spirit
you come and kindle a burning light in us.
We know well that it is not we
who create this source of light,
but you, the Risen Lord.
To all of us, you give the one thing that matters
and which is hidden from our own eyes:
a peaceful trust in God
and also poverty in spirit,
so that with a great thirst for the realities of God,
we may take the risk of letting you accompany us,
O Christ,
and of accompanying, in our turn,
those whom you entrust to us.

(Prayers by Brother Roger)

Prayer around the Cross and Celebration of the Resurrection

Christians have always commemorated each week the central mystery of their faith: the Paschal mystery, the dying and rising of Christ. This mystery sheds light on our own lives as followers of Jesus, as we constantly 'pass over' with him from doubt and anxiety to confident trust, through little deaths to new beginnings.

This passover with Christ from death to life can be celebrated each week in two separate prayers held on Friday and Saturday evenings, or else combined in a single service.

Prayer around the Cross is a way of expressing an invisible communion not only with the crucified Jesus but with all who suffer — all the victims of abandonment, abuse, discrimination or torture. The icon of the Cross is laid down flat in the centre of the Church, resting on a couple of low cushions or stools and illuminated by a few candles. While the meditative singing continues (no. 8, 26, 38, 39 or 50) , those who wish come up to the Cross to pray. They can make a gesture, such as placing their forehead on the wood of the Cross, as a sign that they are entrusting silently to Christ all that burdens them as well as the difficulties of other people, both those known personally and those who are far away but are part of the same human family. This prayer reminds us that now, risen from the dead, Christ accompanies every human being in his or her suffering, even when his presence is not recognised. This form of prayer came from some young Christians in Eastern Europe, who celebrate it every Friday evening.

The resurrection of Christ is the promise of our own resurrection, which already begins invisibly here on earth. It can be celebrated by a festival of the light of Christ, which is also a sign of our identity as Christians as children of the light. Upon entering the church, which should be dimly lit, each person receives a small candle. While a song of resurrection is sung (an alleluia or no. 24, 35, 47 or 48), each person's candle is lit, until the whole church is full of light. Perhaps children can help with this lighting. Then, a Gospel of the resurrection can be read, followed by more meditative singing.

Meditative Songs

Singing is one of the most important forms of prayer.
A few words sung over and over again reinforce the
meditative quality of the prayer. They express a basic
reality of faith that can quickly be grasped by the
intellect, and that gradually penetrates the heart and
the whole being. These simple chants also provide a
way of praying when one is alone, during the day or
at night, or even in the silence of one's heart while
one is working.

38

Alleluia

1 Alleluia 4

(Al - le - lu - ia) Al - le - le - lu - ia, al - le - lu - ia, al - le - lu - ia!

2 Alleluia 7

Al - le - lu - ia, al - le - lu - ia, al - le - lu_____ia. Al - le - lu_____ia!

3 Alleluia 11

Al - le - lu - ia, al - le - lu - ia, al - le - lu - ia!_____

(Al - le - lu - ia)

4 Kyrie Eleison 1

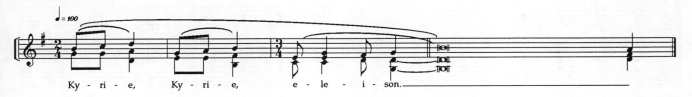

Ky - ri - e,   Ky - ri - e,   e - le - i - son.

5 Kyrie Eleison 10

Ky - ri - e,   Ky - ri - e,   e - le - i - son;   Ky - ri - e,   Ky - ri - e,   e - le - i - son.

6 Kyrie Eleison 13

Ky - ri - e e - lei - son, e - le - i - son.

7

Gospodi

Go - po - di po - mi - luj, Gos - po - di po - mi - luj.

8 Stay with me

Bleibet hier

Blei - bet hier und wa - chet mit mir, Wa - chet und
Stay with me, re - main here mit with me, wat - ching und and

Dm   Gm⁶   Dm   Gm⁶   Dm   C

be - tet, wa - chet und be - tet.
pray - ing, wat - ching und and pray - tet. ing.

F   C   Dm   A⁴ ——— 5

9 **Bless the Lord**

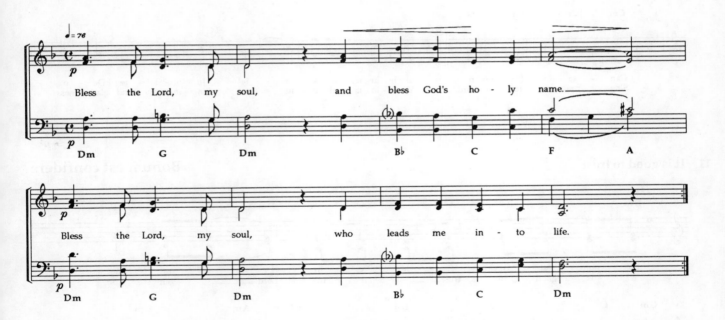

10 Sing praises to the Lord

Cantate Domino

Can - ta - te Do - mi - no. Al - le - lu - ia, al - le - lu - ia! Ju - bi - la - te De - o.
Sing___ prai - ses to the Lord. Al - le - lu - ia, al - le - lu - ia! Sing in joy and glad - ness.

11 It is good to trust

Bonum est confidere

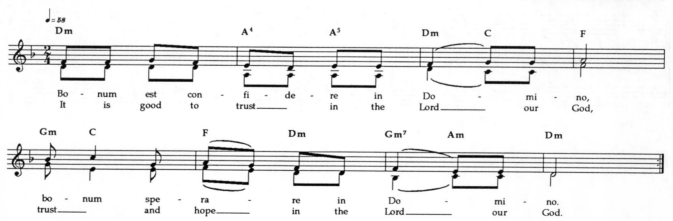

Bo - num est con - fi - de - re in Do - mi - no,
It is good to trust___ in the Lord___ our God,

bo - num spe - ra - re in Do - mi - no.
trust___ and hope___ in the Lord___ our God.

12   **Wait for the Lord**

Lento ♩= 48

p

Wait   for   the   Lord,   whose   day   is   near.

Em   C   Am   B

mf

Wait   for   the   Lord: keep   watch,   take   heart!

Em   D   G   Am   B   Em

44

13 Let us praise your name

Adoremus te Jesu Christe

A - do - re - mus te Je - su Chri - ste, al - le - lu - ia, al - le - lu - ia! Et lau -
Let us praise your Name, God our Sa - viour, al - le - lu - ia, al - le - lu - ia! praise and

de - mus te Je - su Chri - ste, et lau - de - mus te, al - le - lu - ia!
bless your Name, God our Sa - viour, praise and bless your Name, al - le - lu - ia!

14   Our darkness   **La ténèbre**

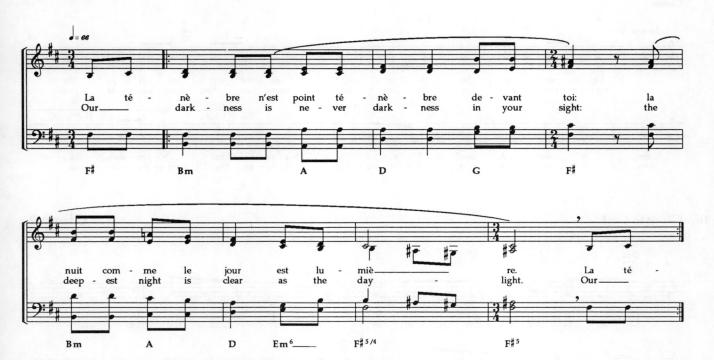

La té - nè - bre n'est point té - nè - bre de - vant toi: la
Our____ dark - ness is ne - ver dark - ness in your sight: the

F♯   Bm   A   D   G   F♯

nuit com - me le jour est lu - miè - - re. La té -
deep - est night is clear as the day - light. Our____

Bm   A   D   Em⁶____ F♯⁵ᐟ⁴   F♯⁵

15 Show us your mercy

Canon

Ostende nobis Domine

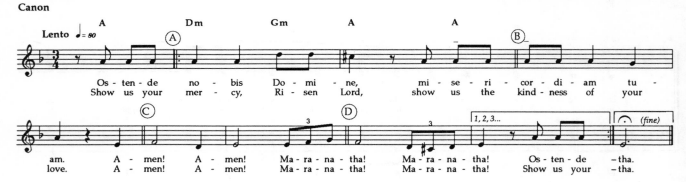

Os - ten - de no - bis Do - mi - ne, mi - se - ri - cor - di - am tu -
Show us your mer - cy, Ri - sen Lord, show us the kind - ness of your

am. A - men! A - men! Ma - ra - na - tha! Ma - ra - na - tha! Os - ten - de -tha.
love. A - men! A - men! Ma - ra - na - tha! Ma - ra - na - tha! Show us your -tha.

16 Glory to God

Canon

Gloria 3

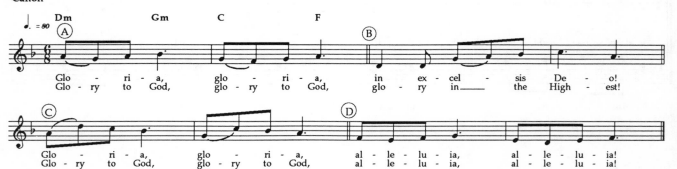

Glo - ri - a, glo - ri - a, in ex - cel - sis De - o!
Glo - ry to God, glo - ry to God, glo - ry in the High - est!

Glo - ri - a, glo - ri - a, al - le - lu - ia, al - le - lu - ia!
Glo - ry to God, glo - ry to God, al - le - lu - ia, al - le - lu - ia!

17　This is the day

48

18 Raise a song of gladness

Jubilate, servite

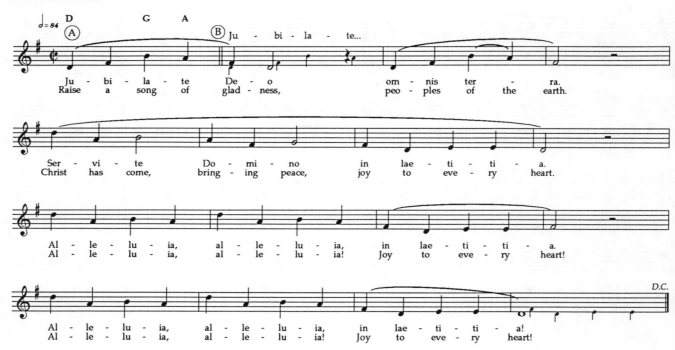

19 In God alone

Mon âme se repose

20   The Lord is my song

O Lord hear my prayer

(a) O Lord hear my prayer, O Lord hear my prayer. When I call an - swer me. O
(b) The Lord is my song, the Lord is my praise: All my hope comes from God. The

Lord hear my prayer, O Lord hear my prayer. Come and lis - ten to me. O
Lord is my song, the Lord is my praise: God, the well - spring of life. The

This tune is sung to words (a) or (b) .

21 **Stay with us**

Bleib mit deiner Gnade

Bleib mit deiner Gnade bei uns, Herr Jesu Christ. Ach,
Stay with us, O Lord Jesus Christ, night will soon fall. Then

bleib mit deiner Gnade bei uns, du treuer Gott.
stay with us, O Lord Jesus Christ, light in our darkness.

22   By your cross

Per Crucem

Canon

Largo ♩ = 96

Per   cru   -   cem   et   pas - si - o - nem   tu - am,
By   your_____   cross   and   all   the   wounds   you   suf - fered,

Li - be - ra nos Do - mi - ne,   li - be - ra nos Do - mi - ne,   li - be - ra nos Do - mi - ne,   Do - mi - ne.
Grant us free - dom in your love,   grant us free - dom in your love,   grant us free - dom in your love,   in   your love.

Per   cru   -   cem   et   pas - si - o - nem   tu - am,
By   your_____   cross   and   all   the   wounds   you   suf - fered,

Li - be - ra nos Do - mi - ne,   li - be - ra nos Do - mi - ne,   li - be - ra nos Do - mi - ne,   Do - mi - ne.
Grant us free - dom in your love,   grant us free - dom in your love,   grant us free - dom in your love,   in   your love.

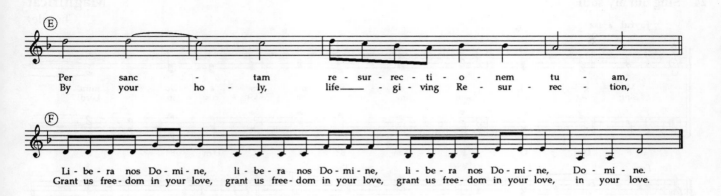

(E)
Per sanc - tam re - sur - rec - ti - o - nem tu - am,
By your ho - ly, life___ gi - ving Re - sur - rec - tion,

(F)
Li - be - ra nos Do - mi - ne, li - be - ra nos Do - mi - ne, li - be - ra nos Do - mi - ne, Do - mi - ne.
Grant us free-dom in your love, grant us free-dom in your love, grant us free-dom in your love, in your love.

23 In the Lord rejoicing

Jubilate Deo

Canon

♩ = 120

(A) (B) (C) (D) (E) (F)
Ju - bi - la - te De - o, Ju - bi - la - te De - o, Al - le - lu - ia!
In the Lord re - joi - cing! Christ is ri - sen from the dead! Al - le - lu - ia!

24 Sing out my soul

Magnificat
(Chorale)

For the solo verses, use the words of the Magnificat (page 14)

E.g. All: Magnificat anima mea Dominum.

Solo: My soul sings praises to the Lord.

All: Magnificat.

Solo: My spirit rejoices in God my Saviour.

All: Magnificat. Magnificat anima mea Dominum.

25

When the night be - comes_____ dark, your love, O Lord,

Em   Am⁶   E   Am   E

is   a   fire;   your love,   O   Lord,   is   a   fire.

Am   E   C⁶   Dm   C   F⁶   E   Am

26 We adore you, Lord Jesus Christ   **Adoramus te Domine**

27 Blessing and praise   **Benedictus**

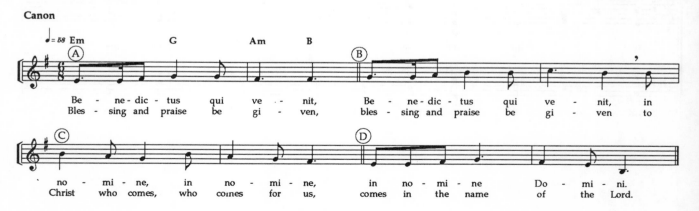

28 Come and fill

Confitemini Domino

Con - fi - te - mi - ni   Do - mi - no   quo - ni - am___   bo - nus.
Come and fill   our hearts with your peace.   You a - lone, O Lord, are ho - ly.

D   Bm   D   A

Con - fi - te - mi - ni   Do - mi - no,   Al - le - lu - ia!
Come and fill   our hearts with your peace, Al - le - lu - ia!

Em   C   Em   A   D

29 Nothing can trouble

Nada te turbe

Na - da   te   tur - be,   na - da   te es - pan - te.   Quien   a   Dios   tie - ne
No - thing   can   trou - ble,   no - thing   can   frigh - ten   those   who   seek   God   shall

Am   Dm⁷   G   Em/C   F   Dm⁶

na - da   le   fal - ta.   So - lo   Dios   bas - ta.
ne - ver   go   want - ing.   God   a - lone   fills   us.

E   Am   F   Dm⁶   E   Am

30 Lord of all goodness

Domine Deus

Do - mi - ne De - us Fi - li - us Pa - tris, do - na no - bis pa - cem.
Lord of all good - ness, Son of the Fa - ther, may your peace sur - round us.

31 Give us your peace

Dona nobis pacem Domine

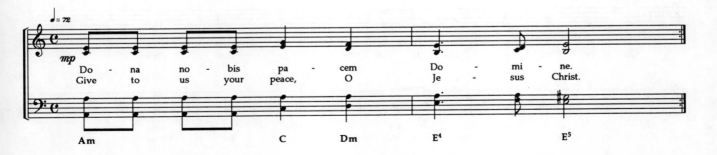

Do - na no - bis pa - cem Do - mi - ne.
Give to us your peace, O Je - sus Christ.

32 Christ Jesus

O Christe Domine Jesu

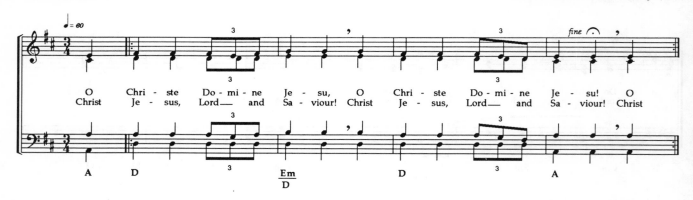

O Christe Domine Jesu, O Christe Domine Jesu! O
Christ Jesus, Lord— and Sa-viour! Christ Je-sus, Lord— and Sa-viour! Christ

A   D   Em/D   D   A

33 Glory be to you

Gloria tibi Domine

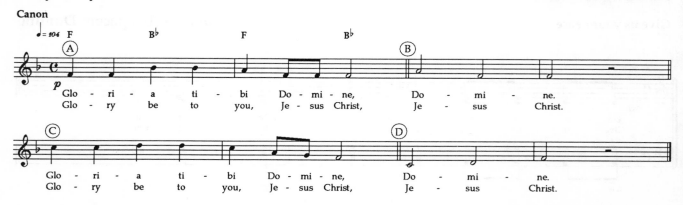

Glo — ri — a ti — bi Do — mi — ne, Do — mi — ne.
Glo — ry be to you, Je — sus Christ, Je — sus Christ.

Glo — ri — a ti — bi Do — mi — ne, Do — mi — ne.
Glo — ry be to you, Je — sus Christ, Je — sus Christ.

34   Spirit of Christ Jesus

Spiritus Jesu Christi

Spi - ri - tus Je - su Chri - sti, Spi - ri - tus ca - ri - ta - tis, con -
Spi - rit of Christ___ Jes - us, Spi - rit of lo - ving kind - ness, con -

fir - met cor___ tu - um; con - fir - met cor___ tu - um.
firm your heart and keep it; con - firm your heart and keep it.

35 Sing, praise and bless the Lord

Laudate Dominum

Lau - da - te Do - mi - num, Lau - da - te Do - mi - num om - nes
Sing, praise and bless the Lord. Sing, praise and bless the Lord, peo - ples!

Am   E   Am   G   C

gen - tes,   Al - le - lu - ia!   Al - le - lu - ia!
na - tions!   Al - le - lu - ia!   Al - le - lu - ia!

G   Am F Dm E   Am Dm E Am

36 **Theme I**   **The Lord is my light**

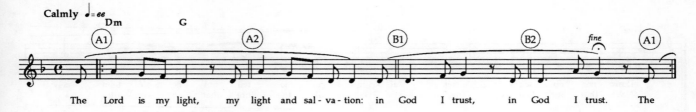

The Lord is my light, my light and sal - va - tion: in God I trust, in God I trust. The

Theme II

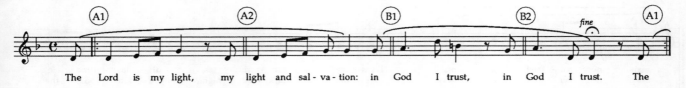

The Lord is my light, my light and sal - va - tion: in God I trust, in God I trust. The

Each of the two themes can be sung *separately* either **in unison** or **as a round** (two voices only : coming in on A1 and B1)
The two themes can also be sung *together*, preferably with theme I for female and theme II for male voices.

37 Within our darkest night

Dans nos obscurités

Dans nos ob - scu - ri - tés al - lu - me le feu qui ne s'é - teint ja -
Wi - thin our dark - est night, you kin - dle the fire that ne - ver dies a -

B   Em   Em   D

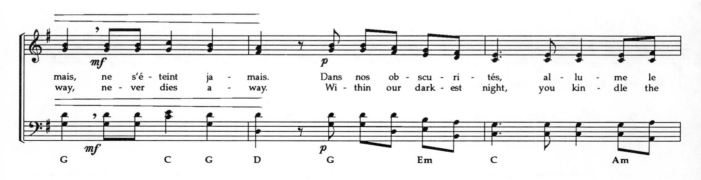

mais, ne s'é - teint ja - mais. Dans nos ob - scu - ri - tés, al - lu - me le
way, ne - ver dies a - way. Wi - thin our dark - est night, you kin - dle the

G   C   G   D   G   Em   C   Am

feu qui ne s'é - teint ja - mais, ne s'é - teint ja - mais. Dans nos ob - scu - ri -
fire that ne - ver dies a - way, ne - ver dies a - way. Wi - thin our dark - est

B   Em   Am   B   Em   Am   B

My soul is at rest
(Psalm 62)

My soul is at rest ___ in God a - lone, my sal - va - tion comes from God. My

A   Dm   A⁴⁻⁵   Dm   C   F   C   Dm   A   Dm   A

39   We adore you, Jesus Christ

Adoramus te Christe

qui - a per cru - cem tu - am re - de - mi - sti mun - dum.
tru - ly your cross and pas - sion bring us life and hea - ling.

A   F♯m   Bm   C♯   A   B   C♯   F♯m

Holy Spirit, loving Spirit

Veni Creator Spiritus

Canon

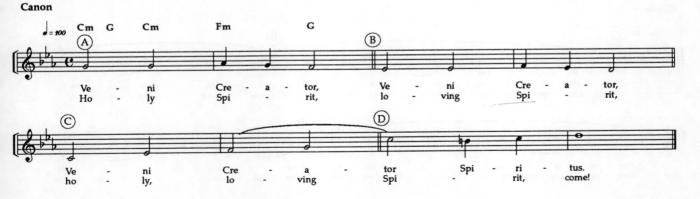

Ve - ni Cre - a - tor, Ve - ni Cre - a - tor,
Ho - ly Spi - rit, lo - ving Spi - rit,

Ve - ni Cre - a - tor Spi - ri - tus.
ho - ly, lo - ving Spi - rit, come!

41 Holy Spirit, come to us

Veni Sancte Spiritus

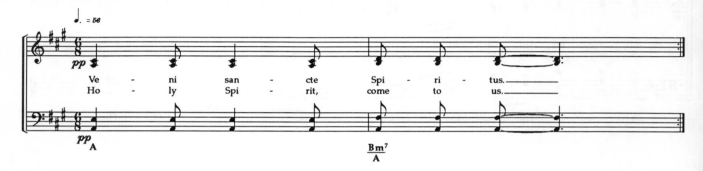

Ve - ni san - cte Spi - ri - tus.
Ho - ly Spi - rit, come to us.

42 Come and pray in us

Vieni, Spirito Creatore

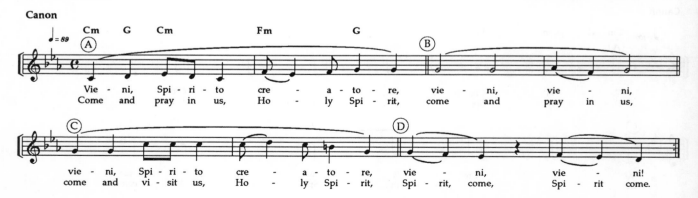

Vie - ni, Spi - ri - to cre - a - to - re, vie - ni, vie - ni,
Come and pray in us, Ho - ly Spi - rit, come and pray in us,

vie - ni, Spi - ri - to cre - a - to - re, vie - ni, vie - ni!
come and vi - sit us, Ho - ly Spi - rit, Spi - rit, come, Spi - rit come.

3 **Holy is the name of God**

Sanctum nomen Domini

44 Give peace

Da pacem cordium

Canon

Da pa - cem cor - di - um. Da pa - cem cor - di - um. Da
Give peace to ev-e - ry heart. Give peace to ev-e - ry heart. Give

pa - - - - - cem. Da pa - - - - - cem. Da
pea - - - ce, Lord. Give pea - - - - ce, Lord. Give

45 Sing out my soul

Magnificat

Canon

Ma - gni - fi - cat. Ma - gni - fi - cat. Ma - gni - fi - cat a - ni - ma me - a Do - min - num.
Sing out, my soul. Sing out, my soul. Sing out and glo - ri - fy the Lord who sets us free.

Ma - gni - fi - cat. Ma - gni - fi - cat. Ma - gni - fi - cat a - ni - ma me - a!
Sing out, my soul. Sing out, my soul. Sing out and glo - ri - fy the Lord God!

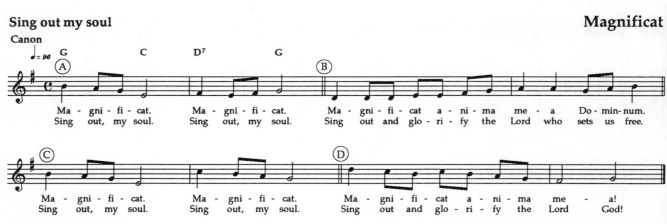

By night

De noche iremos

47 **In the Lord**   **El Senyor**

El Se- nyor és la me-va for- ça, el Se- nyor el me-u cant. Ell m'ha e- stat la sal-va-ci-
In the Lord I'll be ev- er thank-ful, in the Lord I will re- joice! Look to God, do not be a-

Dm C   F   B♭ C   F   C   B♭   A

ó. En ell con- fi- o, i no tinc por. En ell con- fi- o, i no tinc por. El Se-
fraid; lift up your voi- ces, the Lord is near; lift up your voi- ces, the Lord is near. In the

Dm   C   F   B♭   C   Am   Dm   B♭ C F   Dm C

Sing praises

Laudate omnes gentes

49 Living charity

Ubi caritas

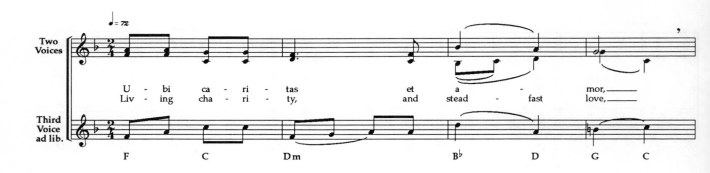

U – bi ca – ri – tas   et   a   –   mor,_____
Liv – ing cha – ri – ty,   and   stead – fast   love,_____

F   C   Dm   B♭   D   G   C

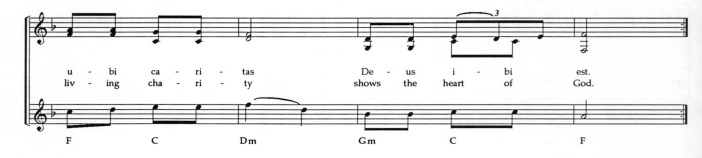

u – bi ca – ri – tas   De – us   i – bi   est.
liv – ing cha – ri – ty   shows the heart of God.

F   C   Dm   Gm   C   F

O Lord, your cross

Crucem tuam

Cru – cem tu – am a – do – ra – mus Do – mi – ne, re – sur – rec – ti – o – nem
O Lord, your cross, we a – dore and glo – ri – fy, for your ho – ly re – sur –

tu – am lau – da – mus Do – mi – ne. Lau – da – mus et glo – ri – fi – ca – mus.
rec – tion, we praise you Lord of life. We praise you and we glo – ri – fy you.

Re – sur – rec – ti – o – nem tu – am lau – da – mus Do – mi – ne. Cru – cem tu –
For your ho – ly re – sur – rec – tion, we praise you Lord of life. O Lord, your

(fine)

Some practical suggestions

Arranging the church or room for prayer

When possible, meet for prayer in a church, making it as welcoming and beautiful as you can.

When no church is available, create a space conducive to a meditative prayer. This can be done using a few simple objects — a cross, an icon or an open Bible, candles and perhaps flowers. Arrange some mats or a carpet for those who wish to kneel or sit on the floor, and benches or chairs behind or around the side for those who prefer. The lighting should be indirect and restful, not too bright.

When we pray all facing the same way, rather than sitting in a circle, we are reminded that we are seeking Christ; our prayer is not centred on ourselves.

The singing

The songs proposed in this booklet are easily learned and are simple enough to be accessible to all kinds of groups.

If they are begun spontaneously, the tone is often too low. It helps to use a tuning-fork or a flute to give the first note or as an accompaniment.

A very effective way of singing the canons (rounds) is for the male voices to start all together and then for the female voices to join in canon, or vice versa.

When teaching the songs be attentive to the rhythm, making sure that they do not drag.

The person teaching the songs should do this apart from the prayer, so that there are no distractions. He or she should not conduct during the prayer itself, so that everyone can focus on the cross or the altar.

Because of the many languages spoken by those present in Taizé, some chants were composed in Latin. They are a link with all the people, in many other countries, who are singing the same songs.

Index of Songs

AS A COMPANION TO THIS BOOK

SONGS AND PRAYERS FROM TAIZÉ: CASSETTE

Recorded at St Paul's, Clifton, Bristol, UK, and in an interpretation which can readily be used in parishes and groups, the cassette presents a number of the songs which appear in this book.

Ireland and UK: Geoffrey Chapman Mowbray, Stanley House, Fleets Lane, Poole BH15 3AJ.

Canada and USA: GIA, 7404 S. Mason Avenue, Chicago, IL 60638.

Australia and New Zealand: Rainbow Book Agencies, 134 Emmaline Street, PO Box 58, Northcote, Vic 3070.

OTHER MUSIC CASSETTES FROM TAIZÉ:

Canons et litanies — Cantate (also on CD) —
Resurrexit (also on CD) — *Alleluia* (also on CD)

Australia and New Zealand: Rainbow Book Agencies.

Canada and USA: GIA.

Ireland and UK: All main stores. Distribution: Redemptorist Publications, Alphonsus House, Chawton, Alton GU3 3HQ.

OTHER MUSIC BOOKS FROM TAIZÉ

Music from Taizé — Two volumes. Vocal and instrumental editions.

Australia: Dove Communications, PO Box 316, Blackburn, Vic 3130.

UK: Collins Liturgical, Westerhill Road, Bishopbriggs, Glasgow G64 2QT

USA: GIA.

VIDEOS:

Taizé — Trust is at Hand
28 minutes VHS PAL video-cassette.
The community and the Intercontinental Meetings, both in Taizé and elsewhere - in European capitals, Madras, Brother Roger at UNESCO, etc.
Australia and New Zealand: Rainbow Book Agencies.
UK: Geoffrey Chapman Mowbray.

Europe: Awakened from Within
24 minutes VHS PAL video-cassette
The Taizé European Meeting which brought together 50,000 young people in Wrocław, Poland, provides a unique view on the European family. This video shows how such a meeting brings to light the special contribution the young can make as Europe searches for its new identity.
Presses de Taizé, F - 71250.

also:

The Letter from Taizé
Every two months, in fifteen languages; news of the Pilgrimage of Trust from across the world, themes for group reflection, texts for meditation, prayers and daily Bible readings.
Subscriptions: write to 71250 Taizé Community, France.

About Taizé

The Story of Taizé
J. L. González Balado
Australia and New Zealand: Mowbray.
Canada and USA: The Liturgical Press, St John's
Abbey, Collegeville, MN 56321.
Ireland and UK: Geoffrey Chapman Mowbray.

The Taizé Experience
A book of photographs by Vladimir Sichov with texts
by Brother Roger
Australia and New Zealand: Geoffrey Chapman
Mowbray.
Canada and USA: The Liturgical Press.
Ireland and UK: Geoffrey Chapman Mowbray.

No Greater Love: Sources of Taizé
Brother Roger of Taizé
'This short book contains what is perhaps the secret of
this extraordinary adventure of faith.'
Australia and New Zealand: Geoffrey Chapman
Mowbray.
Canada and USA: The Liturgical Press.
Ireland and UK: Geoffrey Chapman Mowbray.

His Love is a Fire
Central writings with extracts from journals
Brother Roger of Taizé
Australia and New Zealand: St Paul Publications,
60 Broughton Road, Homebush, NSW 2140.
Canada and USA: The Liturgical Press.
UK: Geoffrey Chapman Mowbray.

Life from Within
Prayers by Brother Roger and icons from the Church
of Reconciliation
Australia and New Zealand: Geoffrey Chapman
Mowbray.
Ireland and UK: Geoffrey Chapman Mowbray.
USA: Westminster / John Knox Press.

Mary Mother of Reconciliations
Mother Teresa of Calcutta and Brother Roger of Taizé
Australia and New Zealand: St Paul Publications.
Ireland and UK: Mowbray.
USA: Paulist Press, Mahwah, NJ.

Meditations on the Way of the Cross
Mother Teresa of Calcutta and Brother Roger of Taizé
Ireland and UK: Mowbray.
USA: The Pilgrim Press.

Mowbray and Geoffrey Chapman Mowbray books
are distributed by:
Australia: Canterbury Press Ltd, Unit 2,
7 Rusdale Street, Scoresby, Vic 3179.
Canada: Meakin Associates, Unit 17, 81 Auriga Drive,
Nepean, Ontario K2E 7Y5.
Malta: Bookport Associates, Casella Postale,
40040 Vado (Bo), Italy.
New Zealand: Hodder & Stoughton, PO 3858,
Auckland 1.
South Africa: Century Hutchinson, PO 337 Bergvlei,
20125.